LONDON TRANSPORT

Buses and Coaches

1949

LONDON TRANSPORT
BUSES & COACHES

1949

John A. S. Hambley

Published 1991 by
The Self Publishing Association Ltd
Lloyds Bank Chambers
Upton-upon-Severn,
Worcs.
A MEMBER OF

in conjunction with
JOHN A.S. HAMBLEY
7 Linden Road,
Dunstable,
Beds. LU5 4NZ

British Library Cataloguing in Publication Data
Hambley, John A.S.
  London Transport: buses & coaches 1949.
  1. London (England). Buses. History
  I. Title
  629.2223309421

ISBN 1 85421 122 6

Designed and Produced by The Self Publishing Association Ltd
Printed and Bound in Great Britain by Tewkesbury Printing Company

Acknowledgements

In assisting me to get this new series of publications launched, I should like to thank the following:

James Aston, Ronald G. Bristow, C. Carter, Alan B. Cross, A.J. Francis, John C. Gillham, D.W.K. Jones, Kevin Lane, S.E. Letts, J.H. Price, Dave Ruddom, Jan Rochford, Saunders Shipbuilding & Engineering Co., now Laird (Anglesey) Ltd., John Smith of Lens of Sutton, John G.S. Smith, Sheila Taylor of the London Transport Museum, S.N.J. White and last but not least my wife Iris who has lived with a transport enthusiast for the past 30 plus years and who has helped in so many ways. Special thanks are also needed for the many unnamed enthusiasts who have given me words of encouragement to carry on. I should also like to thank the PSV Circle who so unreservedly gave me permission to use information from their excellent range of publications dealing with London Transport, which included Class Histories, the yearly 'L' series and their monthly Newsheet.

Publisher's Note:

I would like to ask that if you feel you have suitable pictures of London's buses and coaches in any guise, please do not hoard them, but let others interested in the subject see them. Photographs should be clear and of reasonable quality and any notes to help caption them would be most welcome. The publications dealing with the years 1948 and 1950 are now in an advanced state of preparation, with only a few more photographs required to complete them. Opportunity will be taken to update the previous edition when each yearly publication appears in print, therefore I would appreciate any correspondence from interested parties. At the same time all the un-credited pictures which I have used from my personal collection, which has built up over the last 47 years, could be updated with the photographers name if they would care to correspond. I sincerely hope that through the pages of this book some faded memories have been brought back into focus.

Introduction

This publication is the realization of a personal need to document in pictorial form the activities of London Transport buses and coaches for the years that I have been an enthusiast and before my memory begins to fade. To record by means of a yearly presentation, which vehicles were in service and operating on the streets of London and elsewhere, in fact, wherever London's cast off buses and coaches were used to perform extra duties. These were not always to carry passengers in different parts of the British Isles or even abroad, as we shall see as the series of books progresses. It is intended that a photographic publication will be available for each succeeding and preceding year, which will allow all those interested in the subject to have an unfading reminder of what it was all about in those long-gone forgotten days, to follow the history of many classes of vehicles which once pounded the streets of London and are but just a memory now. The aim is to show in photographs London's buses and coaches, in service and in other uses, together with the street scene as it was in the year covered by the publication. It has changed considerably, not least by the type of bus or coach that was on the road at the time but also by the buildings, roads, roadside furniture and dress sense of the pedestrian and passenger alike. Many present areas of London will be unrecognizable in the photographs presented in this and future publications. Roads have been rebuilt with new alignments, new office and tower blocks have gone up all over the capital, especially in the City and East End areas, which were so devastated in World War II. Then there is the continuing process of updating shop fronts to meet the ever changing shopping trends. Many square miles of country fields have also been used to continue the outward growth of London from its central point into the new suburbs. Bus garages have come and gone too, in the period to be covered by the publications, so that many photographs of buses standing inside or out will be unknown by the present generation. Who for instance can pin-point where Athol Street garage used to stand? On the other hand there are some large areas of London which have changed very little over the years and one will be able to recognize these immediately. Some that readily come to mind are the areas around Oxford Street, Piccadilly Circus (at present anyway), Trafalgar Square,

Big Ben, Whitehall, The Law Courts, Fleet Street and The Royal Exchange are but a few.

Moving onto the buses and coaches themselves. It will become apparent that both lower and upper deck window surround areas were still painted white on the older double deck vehicles in service, whilst new deliveries had the top deck window surrounds only painted with a cream relief. The single deck fleet was also so treated with white or cream relief. It was not until 1950 when new deliveries, overhauled and repainted vehicles first appeared with no window relief. Restricted use of the blind apertures was also still the normal practice and again it was not until 1950 when full use of route blinds was to come into fashion. The continuing process of replacement by new post-war vehicles to the worn out fleet continued and during 1949 a total of 750 RT class buses were added to the fleet. These were A.E.C. Regent Mark III chassis with Park Royal bodies, 81 in total and with Weymann bodies there were 420. Saunders supplied 142, with Craven making up the difference of 107. The RTL class, manufactured with Leyland 7RT chassis and bodies by Park Royal totalled 436, with a further 83 bodied by Metro-Cammell. Then there were the first 210 of the newly appointed 8 feet wide London bus, the RTW class, again on Leyland chassis, this time designated 6RT and carrying Leyland produced bodies. All 160 of the ill fated, short lived SRT class were delivered in 1949, these being reconstructed A.E.C. Regent chassis from the older STL class which had new Park Royal bodies mounted onto them. One Guy Arab III with a Guy body was also delivered, this being G436 and last but not least RTC1 appeared, being rebuilt RT97. In all cases, excepting RTC1, the bodies seated 56 passengers and considering the number of chassis and body builder combinations was something of a feat in itself. New single deck vehicles consisted of 77 Leyland PS1 chassis, which were married up to Mann Egerton 31 seat bodies and numbered TD55-131. At the same time as all these new buses were being added to the streets of London, further withdrawals were being made to the LT class, both single and double deck variants, no fewer than 688 were taken out of regular passenger service. The other double deck classes also lost large numbers, the ST losing no fewer than 540 and the STL class a further 328. Incidentally the figures for both the LT and ST class meant the highest number of these two classes being withdrawn in any one year. Other classes were in evidence on the streets of London, but withdrawals of these had not commenced in the year under review. Turning to the single deck classes. 40 more of the T class and 41 of the original 49 CR class were withdrawn.

STL341 parked up with a further two STL and an LT, taking a well earned rest, no doubt, from their duties in the long haul from Morden Underground Station to the Epsom race-course.

TF47 photographed in Judd Street Coach Station, Kings Cross working on route 727, which plied between London and Luton, via Barnet and St Albans. *(D.W.K. Jones)*

(left) Photographed here at Bunns Lane, Mill Hill is STL1261 carrying an ST lookalike body from an ex DST class vehicle. The chassis of STL1260 to STL1263 were specially short and carried standard pre-selective gearboxes, hence the unusual body for an STL. (D.W.K. Jones)

(below) Much change has taken place here over the last few years and Eccleston Bridge is now almost unrecognisable when compared to this view. Park Royal 6Q6 bodied Q213 basking in this June view with not another road vehicle in sight. (A.B. Cross)

(right) Photographed at Watford High Street garage is 'Bluebird' ST1039 being used as a learner bus, which probably accounts for why the bus still carries the white disc painted onto the lower rear end panel. Introduced during the war years to help following drivers with their masked headlamps in what must have been a very dimly lit London of the day. (D.W.K. Jones)

(below) Green liveried T277 working from Bromley Garage (TB) in the latter months of 1949, was in the early part of 1950 withdrawn from service and disposed of to R.L. Daniels of Rainham. Some years later it was used as a caravan at Dunton Green before being burnt on site in 1969. (J.H. Aston)

Standing outside the entrance to Broad Street Station is STL2019 with STL1590 following up behind. (J.H. Aston)

Photographed at Reigate, STL2654 one of the austerity bodied "unfrozen" examples, is seen working from Godstone garage, followed by one of the many Bristols loaned to London Transport during this period.
(Lens of Sutton)

The only LT class vehicle to be converted to a service vehicle namely 921LT was LT951 specially to carry bus-stop shelters, photographed here inside Chiswick Works. (J.C. Gillham)

What a glorious looking vehicle. LTC21 is waiting patiently in the sunshine for its passengers to return before giving them a ride they will not forget. Somebody somewhere thought the ride good enough to warrant the chassis being exported to Spain in 1953. (A.B. Cross)

Grosvenor Gardens, Victoria and little CR42 does its best to reduce the queues. After World War II many of this forty-nine vehicle strength class were to be seen operating around London, helping out in a similar fashion.

An un-renovated LT1125 from Sutton Garage waits in the sunshine at Belmont Station before returning to Kingston Bus Station on route 213. A minimum fare of two old pence was charged on this route between the Bus Station and Coombe Hill Road as per the slip board notice. (Lens of Sutton)

Carrying out yeoman service right to the end is LT59, on the special service from Morden Station to Epsom racecourse and photographed at Morden. (Lens of Sutton)

Sevenoaks bus station and STL1043 from the first batch of standard front-entrance country area buses, waits happily in the sun. Originally built as a 48 seat vehicle, this was increased to 52 in September 1939.

(Lens of Sutton)

A wintery scene here with Q94 showing the nearside of this type of bus to good advantage, note the very short rear overhang to this side mounted engine bus.

(Lens of Sutton)

Behind Putney Bridge Garage and yet another learner, in the shape of LT1295, taking a rest from its arduous duties. One would have thought that 15 years of serving the public would have been enough, without adding this role onto the end of its life, for over 2 years, before sending it to its ultimate fate, the scrapping yard of Daniels, at Rainham. (Lens of Sutton)

Looking from Coventry Street, past Piccadilly Circus and part way up Regent Street a totally different assortment of buses can be seen, with a Daimler D class, several RT's, including a Craven bodied example and an LT double-deck with several STL type. (London Transport 197)

Finsbury Square looking a little shabby after its wartime experiences, is the background for ex Thomas Tilling ST1027, resuscitated to help out in the post-war vehicle shortage. Here it has found its way on to Route 21 from Old Kent Road (P) Garage. (C. Carter)

C60 sits in the midday sun on the forecourt of Amersham Garage, awaiting its driver perhaps. (D.W.K. Jones)

(right)
The familiar Gillingham Street, Victoria Garage building stands in the background to LT1397 though the photograph is actually taken in Guildhouse Street.
(D.W.K. Jones)

(below)
Q80 photographed on Eccleston Bridge, Victoria, prior to making its long journey out to Luton. It lasted till September 1953 when it was dismantled by LTE.
(A.B. Cross)

(above)
ST10 seen working from Chalk Farm Garage, left for the scrap yard of Daniels, Rainham just a few months later.

(left)
Sydney Road, Muswell Hill and LT31, another open staircased variety, shows off the awkwardly shaped square cab.

(D.W.K. Jones)

LT727 photographed outside the National Provident Institution for Mutual Life Assurance offices, (that's a mouthful) in Gracechurch Street, on a lovely spring-like day, with a full load of passengers, just a few months before being withdrawn from public service. (J.H. Aston)

Epsom racecourse looking rather deserted. Are the crowds still to come, or have they all left for home? ST979 an ex Thomas Tilling vehicle carries a fairly good load in this fine view, which clearly shows the lines of these non-standard LTE Tilling bodied buses. (J.H. Aston)

A very common sight on route 65 at the time were these LGOC 60 seat box-shaped bodied STLs, here STL20 working from Turnham Green Garage waits in the spring sunshine. (J.H. Aston)

Photographed here on a short working of Route 362 is 17STL3/3, green STL2663, which later finished its days with London Transport firstly as a training vehicle and later as a staff bus, before the chassis was despatched to Beeline Roadways Limited and fitted with a single deck secondhand Strachan body!

(J.H. Aston)

A superb shot of front entrance STL1490, clearly showing the draughty entrance/exit to these Weymann bodied buses. Like most of this batch of 50 vehicles, nobody wanted to operate it when London had finished with them, so off to the scrap yard it was despatched. (D.W.K. Jones)

LT1181 at the Crooked Billet, Penge and what a lovely view, with the old shop fronts, the delivery barrow and that hat of the lady on the right. All help evoke the atmosphere of the time. (J.H. Price)

What a magnificent beast – another "Bluebird" type, LT1403 is photographed at Belmont Station with the Tilling ST Staff Canteen in the background, which was a familiar sight for so long. (Lens of Sutton)

Brand new SRT2 using the chassis from ex STL2520 photographed at Camberwell Garage with an assortment of hired vehicles. (D.W.K. Jones)

STL1527 with B26 in the background, stand in Windmill Lane, Greenford, before departing their separate ways. (J.C. Gillham)

LT646 on route 105 at Park Royal Station, note the deserted streets save for just three cars. (J.H. Price)

ST1104 in green livery, standing in the forecourt of Victoria railway station on a very dismal February day. The square box cab and lack of side indicator on its Ransome's body indicate the vehicle's East Surrey origins. Plenty of new RT's in the background but the ST only has six months left in service, prior to being scrapped by Daniels of Rainham. (A.B. Cross)

Here a brand new RTW32 with another unidentifiable example parked up behind are caught by the camera. (J.H. Aston)

ST466 with a 11T11 just about to overtake, photographed in Hounslow. The ST was one of a number loaned to B.M.M.O. during some of the war years. (A.B. Cross)

(left) Photographed in Kennington, RTC1 in its short lived role as a Green Line coach looks very handsome, when compared to LT477 following on behind. (D.W.K. Jones)

(below) The lovely looking Royal Forest Hotel, Chingford makes a pleasant stand for buses on routes which served this historic watering hole. Here G399, a Weymann bodied example, stands next to G302 an N.C.M.E. bodied bus which later went to Edinburgh Corporation, to be rebodied. G399 was also rebodied by its new owners, Transportes, Jardine-Galder, of Gran Canaria. (A.B. Cross)

A brand new Craven bodied RT1445. These had more windows along the length of the vehicle than any other manufacturers products, so they were easily the most obvious to identify of the RT family type. (A.B. Cross)

A rather standard ST125, no glorious past in its history you can say, except for serving Londoners for slightly over 19 years.

STL1009B A superb alternative arrangement for passengers to board and alight was provided with these front entrance double-deckers, although it was very draughty with no doors being fitted to keep passengers happy. This STL ended its days with Wilson Lovatt the National Contractor from London.

(A.B. Cross)

Epping Town provides the setting for T524, about to begin its long haul to Windsor. (C. Carter)

Ex Tilling ST917 now mobile canteen 691J photographed here at Uxbridge (UX) Garage. (J.C. Gillham)

C39 is one of 74, 2C2 type vehicles bodied by Short Brothers (Rochester and Bedford) Limited, another 22 similar buses were bodied by Weymann. (J.C. Gillham)

Seen here at Amersham Garage is STL2670, a 17STL12/1 now carrying Country Area colours, but originally delivered in wartime red livery. Ended its days with London Transport first as a staff bus and later as a training vehicle. (Lens of Sutton)

Wembley High Road and roof box STL2267 does business with the general public, having still around a year of its life left carrying out similar duties.

G176 with Massey bodywork working from Barking Garage, one of a handful of garages which played host to this type of vehicle all their working life in London, eventually spent its later years at Aldermaston with A.W.R.E. (C. Carter)

RT417 with a renovated single deck LT standing in sight behind it. The RT was one of the first Weymann bodied examples to be delivered, way back in 1947. (J.H. Aston)

Newly overhauled D171 stands in the sunshine on the south-east side of Chiswick Works, ready for a few more years service. (J.C. Gillham)

Now this is what I call a real caravan, the top deck of an STL from the batch STL203-608 mounted on a 'new' chassis and with a door-way having been added half way along the side. Towed around by a vehicle bearing the number LVX 920, but photographed here in a static condition at Canvey Island. They just do not make caravans like they used to, do they? (J.C. Gillham)

The driver training school at Chiswick Works provides the resting place for ST218 and LT762 both of which are now used in the capacity as learners. (J.C. Gillham)

Wells Terrace, Finsbury Park and LT1164, a renovated example leaves on its Muswell Hill journey. (Lens of Sutton)

The George, Crawley and STL1952 sits in the warm sunshine of this Sussex town. (D.W.K. Jones)

Another special working. This time the Wimbledon Tennis Grounds to Wimbledon Station service, and again an older vehicle, in the shape of LT42, an open staircase variety performs. As in another picture, special Slazenger advertisements seem to have been applied. (Lens of Sutton)

T359 photographed at Wells Terrace, Finsbury Park, carries the Weymann 30 seat bus body of ex R26. The original Strachan coach body was scrapped at the time of rebodying, in 1938. The first bridge in the background, on the site of the present bus station, gave rail access to the coal-yard on the left. (A.B. Cross)

Working from Epping on route 720, and seen at Aldgate, is TF32, a few years before it was dismantled by the Executive. (J.H. Aston)

Post-war STL2690 is captured here at Uxbridge Underground Station, six years before all 20 of the sub-class 18STL20's were disposed of to North of Leeds, for further service with a number of Corporations. (J.H. Aston)

SRT6 photographed at Aldgate, used the 15STL sub-type chassis of ex STL2540 to produce this short lived vehicle. The Park Royal body from SRT6 was later used in the production of RT4437. (J.H. Aston)

Another ex bus, this time STL175, but now known as service vehicle 739J. Note this vehicle still keeps both its dumb iron identification brass plates. Standing to its right is stores lorry 397W which was once T257.

(Lens of Sutton)

Windmill Road, Greenford and STL560 with one of the mobile staff canteens in the background, in this case 689J which was once ST969, having been converted for this new role in 1946. The poster for Shepherds Bush Empire reminds us that television had not yet destroyed the Variety Theatre.   (J.H. Aston)

(right) ST802 repainted into green livery in 1945 and photographed in this guise at Morden Underground Station in accompaniment with D class vehicles, which were prolific at the time in this area. (A.B. Cross)

(below) STL1190 having been repainted from red in May 1941 and operating from the now closed High Wycombe Garage. It is pictured at Uxbridge Underground Station. The restricted destination blinds show the standard wartime Country Area practice. (A.B. Cross)

(above) Pictured here at Sevenoaks Bus Station is T441, one of 50 such 9T9 vehicles all of which were converted to public ambulances during World War II, this T later moving onto the U.S. authorities. (A.B. Cross)

(left) Epsom Railway Station and at least three ST's, leading with 979, await their turn to take horse-racing fans the long journey to the racecourse.

Photographed inside Chiswick Works in company with a number of loaned Bristols, a G Class vehicle and an ST, is this 8 feet wide test rig for RTW route evaluation, made up of a normal AEC Regent Mark III chassis and part of an RT type body with additional structural work. Its extra width can easily be distinguished by careful inspection of the vehicle. The wheel and tyre assembly on the front axle has been turned around, and the rear wheels are set in further underneath the side panelling than is normal. The complete vehicle was known by its chassis number 0961037 which, once the experiment had been completed, formed the basis of RT2436 when fitted with a new Weymann body in December 1949. (D.W.K. Jones)

Another shot of an unfrozen STL taken on route 411, this time though STL2672. The trees in the background are now completely filled out and full of greenery unlike the earlier wintry shot of STL2654. (J.H. Aston)

Another renovated single decker, photographed at Belmont Station, this time LT1148, which went away to Cambridge in August 1948, not returning back to London till February the following year. (A.B. Cross)

LT1033 renovated, but looking a little sad around the engine compartment area. Standing in the sunshine at the Uxbridge bus terminus, which is totally unrecognisable nowadays. (A.B. Cross)

451W a stores lorry, but underneath the body lies the chassis of ex T160. Until lost in time, these lorry conversions very conveniently kept their dumb iron identification plates, therefore, making the job of finding which bus or coach was used in the conversion that much easier. (D.W.K. Jones)

STL2664 seen here in Chesham, its wartime unfrozen chassis being much younger than its Chiswick float body. With just under two years service left to do in London, before being shipped to the Baghdad Passenger Transport organisation of Iraq. I just wonder what its new owners thought of it! (A.B. Cross)

Duple-bodied D3 from the first batch of lowbridge Daimler CWA6 for route 127 seen here at the South Wimbledon Station terminus of this service.

(E.G.P. Masterman via A.J. Francis)

ST1034 one of the famous "Bluebird" sub-class of vehicle which always carried green livery. They were acquired from London General Country Services, Reigate in July 1933 and this one was scrapped the month after being photographed. Interestingly, this was the only 3ST4 to be converted to operate on producer gas during World War II. (A.B. Cross)

ST645 seen here in Fulham Palace Road is another standard ST, which departed for the scrap yard before the end of the year.

Parked in the Chiswick Works grounds with a few STL's and G310 is LTC1 which shows its sunshine roof which was carried by fourteen out of the twenty four of the class. (J.C. Gillham)

Originally an ex Amersham and District Motor Bus and Haulage Company Limited vehicle. Much changed as it now carries a Weymann body; replacing its Strachan example carried till November 1938 and an oil engine in place of the original petrol one. The scenic background is Alexandra Palace. (D.W.K. Jones)

In the August sunshine at Rickmansworth, stands T283 with plenty of scratches along it from roadside trees and bushes, I expect. (D.W.K. Jones)

Alexandra Palace provides the backdrop for Q143 a Park Royal bodied bus, one of eighty such vehicles delivered back in 1936. Sadly the bus was one of many cut up by Bollands (breakers) of Wakefield in the mid-fifties. (D.W.K. Jones)

T759 a Weymann bodied post-war AEC Regal bus, seen here at Uxbridge Underground Station working from Uxbridge Garage, having started its career from Muswell Hill late in 1946. (D.W.K. Jones)

RTW10 working from its original garage allocation of Tottenham, when only a few weeks with the Executive. This type of bus, were the first 8 feet wide buses used by London Transport. (J.H. Aston)

STL1724 rebuilt by an organisation called Rowlls Limited, of Hereford, between August 1944 and February 1945. One can only assume that it must have been in a bad state to need seven months attention given to it. The bus was scrapped in 1950, though it does in this photograph appear to be happy at work here on the Sunday 27B route, operating from Holloway Garage.

ST850 helping out, seen here at Epsom Racecourse. Many LT's and ST's performed these duties in the year under review, before being delicenced and disposed of. (J.H. Aston)

(left) Chiswick Works forms the back drop to this shot of the front end of ex bus, NY12 originally Peoples of Hertford and Ware. This Thorneycroft Cygnet chassis was used in 1935 for the basis of stores lorry 335T. (D.W.K. Jones)

(below) Q55 seen on Eccleston Bridge, works from East Grinstead Garage. This vehicle was lucky to be the Q type LTE kept as a museum piece. (A.B. Cross)

(right) C26 photographed at Orpington Station, was originally one of the 12 Country area buses which were repainted red during 1942, only 10 of which, including this one were repainted back into green livery in 1948. This could account for the quite good condition it appears to be in. The chassis only was noted at Lancashire Motor traders, a dealer of Salford in 1956/7. (A.B. Cross)

(below) Sevenoaks provides us with STL1475, another front entrance bus but this time a Weymann bodied example still with 48 seats followed by T427. (Lens of Sutton)

A wet and windy day at Victoria Station, but the conductor of ST458 does not seem to mind. This was a "strange working" on 76, normally the province of Guys.

Brand new TD43 appears to be suffering the same problem as motorists always have, picking up the mess from the road surface. At least it has ten years of such service to look forward too, before going to an even dustier environment, namely Ceylon. Potters Bar forecourt provides its resting place for the camera of D.W.K. Jones.
(D.W.K. Jones)

Photographed at Otter Road, Greenford is STD167 an all Leyland product, which lasted till 1955 in London, it is thought to have been exported to Yugoslavia together with the rest of the sub type 4STD3 vehicles. (J.C. Gillham)

T314 A lovely front end view of an ex Thomas Tilling bus, (one of twelve such vehicles) helping out on Route 16 from Cricklewood in early post-war years and photographed at Victoria, but not for much longer as in August it left for Rainham to be scrapped. (A.B. Cross)

Finsbury Square and RT901 a Park Royal bodied example.

LT881 seen in a later photograph, but here puts in
what must be one of its last duties on the
Morden-Epsom Racecourse special
service. In September it was
withdrawn from
service.

ST2 seen at Kingston with just four months revenue earning service left to do before as was usual at this time, it
made its way to Rainham. (J.H. Aston)

The boiler house inside Chiswick Works provides the background here to C113. Channel Islands Airways is carried in the side mounted information box. (J.C. Gillham)

Here in red (central area) livery is ST1108, operating from Dalston (D) Garage and photographed standing on the cobbles outside Shepherds Bush (S) Garage awaiting its duty on route 11.
(J.C. Gillham)

Just delivered G436 complete with paper sticker announcing body builders, photographed inside Chiswick Works. This was the last Guy Arab to be delivered to the Executive. (J.C. Gillham)

Ex Lewis Omnibus Company Limited AEC Regal, later T363 but here photographed operating for the Paddington Transport Service, at Southend-on-Sea. (J.C. Gillham)

Not quite what at first it appears to be as Ex LPTB DST6 is a Daimler CH6 chassis, but now fitted with an AEC engine and radiator. When photographed at the Southend-on-Sea Kursaal Coach Park (now that brings back memories) the vehicle was being operated by M. Leader, of Stratford, London. (J.C. Gillham)

One of the Park Royal bodied variety of 5Q5 caught here at Eltham. Q166 is from the batch of 80 which have entrances forward of the front wheels.

Brand new TD117, Leyland PS1 chassis with Mann Egerton 31 seat bus body, working from Leyton Garage and caught by the camera in Wick Road, Hackney.

Red STL1683 operating as a Green Line relief must have seemed a very poor ride to its passengers when compared to the normal single deck coach used on route 704 at the time. Tunbridge Wells Garage code plate is carried in its holder with a chalked on running number. (A.B. Cross)

Photographed at St Paul's Church Yard is T262, originally built as a Green Line coach it still carries its green livery although having been transferred permanently to the Central Area. (J.H. Aston)

At Aldgate, waiting to depart for its journey to Camberwell Green is LT881, being one of many double-deck LT's to be renovated by Mann Egerton of Norwich. (A.B. Cross)

Belmont Station again. Another favourite spot for photographers in the period covered by this book. LT1159 leaving for its home garage base, Kingston. (Lens of Sutton)

A nice low frontal view of an unrenovated LT1095 pictured at Mill Hill East. (D.W.K. Jones)

Another view of an LGOC bodied bus, seating 60 passengers. STL43 awaits its turn on route 7 at Kew Green. (D.W.K. Jones)

Tilling T314 resting in the sun at Page Street, Mill Hill, gives a chance for the conductor to have a few words with the driver. (D.W.K. Jones)

(above) LT1427 the sister to LT1428 but operating in another part of London, at the time. Photographed at the Crooked Billet, Penge.
(A.B. Cross)

(left) Another shot of this lovely class of vehicle, LTC12, photographed, this time at St Paul's Cathedral on a private hire, organised by Dean and Dawson. (J.H. Aston) *(right)* T280 photographed at Uxbridge Bus Station, one of the 11T11s which were T's re-bodied with Weymann bodies from the old R class type of vehicle. (A.B. Cross)

(below) A much travelled LT349 was renovated by Mann Egerton of Norwich in the early part of 1946, having previously been repaired by Cardiff Corporation in an exercise which took nine months from August 1944. The result was a rather unusual looking top deck. (A.B. Cross)

T264 is beginning to look a little sad for itself, but somebody has chalked OK on the radiator, though looking at the contents of the yard one does not have much hope for it.

T594 one of the twelve 10T10's not returned to LPTB by the American Authorities after hostilities ceased in 1945. Looking very pleased with itself and new registration BRD 922, it is seen here whilst with Smiths of Reading.

Photographed in Gracechurch Street is ST537 an all together standard product of the time, when built. (J.H. Aston)

Petrol engined LTC20 sits in the glorious sunshine, waiting for the passengers who must enjoy the Windsor tour in this lovely machine, the chassis of which was eventually exported to Spain. (D.W.K. Jones)

O961079 a post-war AEC Regent Mark III chassis with a suitably modified Tilling body dating from the early 1930 period. Used mainly as a training unit by garages where post-war RT class vehicles were to be delivered, but pictured here outside Croydon Garage which had RTs delivered nearly 2 years earlier. After its job had been completed the body was scrapped and the chassis was used underneath a Weymann body to produce RT4761. (D.W.K. Jones)

In the days before Dundee Corporation put it to work, STL2685 enjoys the sunshine at Rickmansworth, being one of 20 Weymann bodied provincial type post-war double-deckers. (D.W.K. Jones)

STL1593 on route 54 in company with a Bedford OB of Cliffs of Eltham helping out on route 126 and an ST photographed at Beckenham Junction. (J.H. Price)

T215 photographed at Uxbridge Underground Station is another 11T11 conversion being a rebodied AEC Regal chassis with the body ex R31 in this instance, it still had a number of years service with London Transport left to do when this photograph was taken.

ST1137 acquired from the Lewis Omnibus Company Limited of Watford, fleet number R5 and carrying a Short 48 seat body, was rebodied with a familiar ST type body in 1939 and is seen here in York Way, Kings Cross.
(D.W.K. Jones)

Photographed at Chessington Zoo is STL383, one of the standard LPTB bodied buses of the day, this particular one only lasting till the end of the year. (J.H. Aston)

Photographed in Lewisham is STL1867 one of the 40 specially bodied buses built for use through the Blackwall Tunnel, clearly showing the curved roof lines of its LPTB, 55 seat body, one less than the standard bodied bus.

Photographed in Ongar, STL2562. Despite its smart appearance this particular vehicle went to Daniels of Rainham for scrap in under a year after being captured by the camera. (A.B. Cross)

STL60, an original Thomas Tilling Limited bus with Tilling's own bodywork. All of these 7STL4 vehicles were withdrawn from service before the end of the year. (A.B. Cross)

LT1068 did not make it to the renovators, but still made an impressive sight on the roads, even with only four months left in public service. Seen at Uxbridge Underground Station. (A.B. Cross)

(above) RT283 has now been in service for over a year and still operates from its initial allocated Garage, Middle Row (X). Pictured here at Kew Green. (J.H. Aston)

(right) In the yard opposite Watford High Street Garage, post-war STL2697 stands beside STL201, the latter built some 23 years earlier and now demoted to learner duties, which it performed at Addlestone, Watford High Street, and later Victoria before succumbing to the scrap dealer. (D.W.K. Jones)

From the original batch of Guy Arab I chassis with Park Royal bodies, G19 in accompaniment with STL, RT and STD types waits for its turn on route 76 from Victoria Station forecourt.   (J.H. Aston)

Weymann bodied G372 waits in accompaniment with another Guy at Kew Green on the Sunday 83A.

(J.H. Aston)

Marylebone Station and Massey bodied G182 does its stint on route 23, spending its entire passenger revenue earning service at Barking Garage. (J.H. Aston)

Rebuilt and renovated by Marshalls of Cambridge just three months prior to this photograph being taken and T24 already has two panels which have been badly scraped. Viewed at The Fountain, New Malden, Surrey. (A.B. Cross)

T658 looking very attractive in its post-war livery although operating on bus route 458, with Green Line names; still five years away from travelling to Norths at Leeds for scrap, but for now standing in peaceful Uxbridge.

Variety here in the yard on the opposite side of the road from Watford High Street Garage (WA). From left to right are front entrance STL1491, post-war STL2695, brand new Craven bodied RT1413, roof mounted route box STL2006, front entrance STL1493 and another post-war vehicle STL2696.
(D.W.K. Jones)

Windmill Lane, Greenford again, and this time B3 waits its duty on route 97. This vehicle together with most of these 1B1 coded vehicles went onto Crosville Motor Services, Chester in 1953.
(J.C. Gillham)

Early in the year, and RT621 is seen in the yard opposite Watford High Street Garage, in company with two post war STL's.

Acton High Street and STL379 is seen carrying a very sparse number of passengers. This bus later turned up with an unidentified showman once it had finished its London career. (D.W.K. Jones)

(left) STL2513 having just passed underneath the dim looking railway bridge at Romford Station, a fairly typical looking bus of the class, ended its life with London Transport as a trainer vehicle from Turnham Green Garage.

(below) Pictured here at Stroud Green Road, Finsbury Park under the bridge which over the years has decapitated many double-decker is unrenovated LT1074 standing half in shadow, half in sunshine, but clearly showing the front end of this type of single-decker. (A.B. Cross)

(*above*) Q34B photographed in the main St Albans thoroughfare, St Peters Street, four years prior to making its way to the dealer W. North of Leeds. It was later exported to Tripoli, Libya and operated by Unione Tripolina Autotrasporti. (A.B. Cross)

(*right*) LT938 photographed at The Pavement, Clapham Common looking very presentable, when one considers it missed out being renovated or attended to by any of the outside contractors who took this type of work on to keep London's buses on the road.

An unknown STL body, the chassis of which went on to be used as a basis for an SRT type bus. Photographed at the Old Welsh Hospital at Hendon. (J.H. Price)

Taking a well earned rest behind the old Putney Bridge Garage is CR34, which took another rest as a tea hut behind the premises of E. Nuttall, Colnbrook, Buckinghamshire some years later. The hand operate tower wagon in the background is of interest. (Lens of Sutton)

One of the very interesting Park Royal bodied deck and a half, blue and cream liveried Leyland Cubs built for the Inter-Station Service. In this instance C110 waits in the gloom of one of the London termini.

Lowbridge D1 photographed at South Wimbledon Underground Station, was the first of 10 such vehicles for use on Route 127, which needed this type, for a lowbridge at Worcester Park Station. Seating upstairs was 4 abreast with a sunken gangway on the off-side of the body. (Lens of Sutton)

STL2479 working from the old Crawley Garage, with just over a year before leaving for Daniels of Rainham.

The first example of a chassis type which reached 435 vehicles during and just after World War II. G1 is seen here at Victoria Railway Station, with STL, RT and a loaned Bristol all included in the view. (D.W.K. Jones)

Interior shot of TF9, looking forward with sunroof open and showing the superb view, passengers had of the outside world from this coach, it is the only one left after the war from a batch of 12, all the others being destroyed in the disastrous air raid attack on the Bull Yard, Peckham, way back in 1940. (D.W.K. Jones)

LT20 photographed at the Epsom June meeting. Where are all the other cars and buses? This must have been one of its last duties, as it was scrapped later that month.

A fine view of RT77 working from Putney Bridge Garage, which was always associated with this type of vehicle, here pictured at leafy Hampton Court. (J.H. Aston)

Hampton Court and photographed here is RT19, now carrying the modified body ex RT1. In its original condition the bus was used as a demonstrator, and was loaned to various operators by A.E.C. Limited. The body is now carried on the preserved 'RT1' albeit on a later chassis. (J.H. Aston)

Derby Day at Epsom and green liveried ex Tilling STL128 helps moves the crowds, previous it had been in use at Watford, Hight Street Garage (WA) and Tring (TG) Garage. (J.C. Gillham)

Ex bus T320, but now known as overhead wire lubricator 114W, obviously kept some of its LPTB bus parts around the cab area with the addition of a rather narrow cab door for the driver. (Lens of Sutton)

A common enough sight during the war years, but one wonders why after several years of peace, LT1013, minus one window needs to go out on service in such condition. The modern looks of Arnos Grove station exterior contrast sharply with the dated lines of the single-decker. (R.H.G. Simpson)

Another scrap yard view, with at least STL58 and LT1194 awaiting their sad fate. The STL even has an ominously looking "S" in the first window behind the drivers cab.

Photographed at Oxted Police Station is C19, one of a batch of 74 vehicles bodied by Short Brothers (Rochester and Bedford) Limited, for the Country Area, and seating 20 passengers. The bus is one of 10 which at one time were painted red, returning to green livery at various dates. (R. Bristow)

219U, ex bus LS6 standing inside Hammersmith (R) Garage, just enough to warm its very dated frontal appearance up, and I suppose help it to look not quite so ugly. (D.W.K. Jones)

T156 stands at the Western Region Station, Staines, whilst waiting its turn on the 218 route back to Kingston. This was the only 1T1 vehicle built as new with a front entrance. (D.W.K. Jones)

T1 carrying a painted radiator shell. I must admit I cannot remember seeing any like this. Was it to save money over the normally polished variety, one wonders? The bus is photographed here at Sunbury Church. (D.W.K. Jones)

TF9 looking splendid in this view taken at St Pauls Cathedral. The coach later in its life had an all over green livery which did not help it stand out in the crowd, as it does just now. At least it still has four years service in London left to do which will please many hundreds of passengers, and photographers. (D.W.K. Jones)

(left) Another dapper CR, this time CR11 parked at Hornchurch Garage. Dismantled by the LTE after its passenger revenue earning days were over. (A.B. Cross)

(below) Angel Road, Edmonton and ST676 passes the camera, only a few months before it was scrapped by Daniels of Rainham.

(above) ST1101 another former East Surrey vehicle, note the PG registration, in green livery working from Middle Row Garage caught by the camera at the Savoy Cinema, East Acton but with only two months of service left before being scrapped.

(A.B. Cross)

(left) ST674 was one of those ST's to be converted to run on producer gas during 18 months of the war years, looks no worse for its experience from other members of its class in this 1949 shot taken in Dagenham.

A rather deserted Uxbridge Underground Station and Country area T297 waits its turn on Route 458 to Slough at the opposite end of the route to a later photograph of the same bus. Only a few months away from being moved to the Central Area for work at Kingston and Sidcup. In this view can be seen one of the mobile canteens, namely 691J, which was once a Thomas Tilling ST number 917. (A.B. Cross)

Once a Green Line coach with a Ransomes 30 seat coach body, and classified 1/7T7/1, T275 was, in November 1938, rebodied with the body of ex bus R24 and classified 11T11. It is photographed here with T253 behind, at Uxbridge Underground Station. (D.W.K. Jones)

Kingston Railway Station here, provides an interesting shot of T273. The position of the destination box, much higher than other examples in this book, indicate a pre-war bus conversion. The background provides assorted rolling stock which will be of interest to Railway enthusiasts. (D.W.K. Jones)

RT1046 several months after being put into service by Leatherhead Garage, at the Chessington terminus of the 468.

A tranquil view, which includes ST386 here in red livery on a Country area route. (J.H. Aston)

T623 painted in Green Line colours, carries out some Country Area bus duties here on Route 425 from Guildford to Dorking. (J.H. Aston)

LT1159 at Belmont Station was never renovated, so this bus was one of the earlier numbers to be scrapped by Daniels of Rainham in 1949.

Standing in the car and bus park of sunny Chessington Zoo is STL381 with ST614 next and a further unidentifiable ST to its right. (J.H. Aston)

689J, ex ST969 bus, taken in Windmill Road, Greenford. (J.H. Aston)

Park Royal bodied G340 with a Northern
Counties bodied example behind.
(Lens of Sutton)

ST374 on loan to Country Area Reigate Garage from the Central Area with temporary paper route details and
only three months left of its life in public service. Seen here at South Croydon. (A.B. Cross)

Here parked at Chelsham Garage is Q58. One of 75 Birmingham Railway Wagon and Carriage Company Limited bodied AEC Q's.

Acton High Street and ST533 on a warm spring day is one of many of a sub-class, which could be considered the standard of the class. This particular bus was overhauled by Berkeley Caravans, Biggleswade between December 1948 and February 1949.

Leafy Rickmansworth provides the background here to Mann Egerton bodied A.E.C. Regal T791 delivered the previous year. Particular interest should be paid to the manually operated sliding passenger door and, in this view, the unused roof fitting for the route number.

ST501 standing at West Croydon Station, was one of a number loaned to the Caledonian Omnibus Company of Dumfries, during part of the war years. Used as a training bus at the end of its passenger carrying days, it reached Daniels (dealer) of Rainham later in the year.

(*above*) Originally bus NS2322 back in the General days, but ending its time with LTE as a mobile staff canteen, number 3 being numbered 40H in the service vehicle fleet. A very peaceful resting place for all the years of faithful service given. (A.B. Cross)

(*left*) ST671 ended its days as a trainer, just a few miles away at Croydon Garage (TC), soon after being photographed operating out of Catford Garage. Unfortunately, like many of ST Class of vehicle, it was scrapped by Daniels of Rainham.

(right) Amersham Bus Garage provides the photographer with STL 2679 and 2656, numerically very close together but carrying totally different type of bodywork. STL2679 has a STL1/1 LGOC 60 seater body whilst 2656 carries a STL11/1 type, built by the LPTB for 56 seated passengers. Neither vehicle had many months of London service left.

(below) Rickmansworth Station and STL1910 picks up more passengers, in this rural view.

Q89 shows off its very unusual body shape, in this view of the bus at Rickmansworth.

LT1128 one of many which had been renovated by Marshalls of Cambridge, having been attended to between July and December, 1948. (A.B. Cross)

C82 scurrying around Dagenham shows off the neat little package one bought when specifying Weymann 20 seat body to be mounted on a Leyland Cub chassis. This little bus was reported many years later as a showmens winter quarters at Stainforth, Yorkshire.

Two green liveried RT's await here at Kingston Railway Station. RT1067 with RT1071 standing to its left are both Weymann bodied examples. (J.H. Aston)

Once a Green Line coach but now a more humble country bus, seen here at Slough Station. T297 was, during the war years, one of those converted to a staff ambulance along with many others of the class, and was given the ignominious service stock number of 427W. It was one of the last ten of the batch to be withdrawn from passenger service.

STL976 from the first batch of front entrance STL's, carried an LPTB 48 seater body when new, increased to 52 in 1939 by the fitting of four extra seats over the wheel arches. This STL was also rehabilitated by Mann Egerton in 1948, which probably helped it to be one of the last 10STL6 type to be withdrawn.

ST1089 photographed at the Western Region Station at Staines, was once in the possession of Amersham and District Motor Bus and Haulage Company Limited, before being acquird by the Country Area. Its ST coding was 3/1ST9/1 and was the only vehicle to carry this code. (Lens of Sutton)

Cromwell Road, Kingston provides the resting place for T11. Do you think the conductor is wondering why the photographer should want to photograph this bus! (J.C. Gillham)

LT597 seen here at Shoreditch Church has only around six months service left with London Transport before making its way to Daniels, dealers of Rainham. (D.W.K. Jones)

Slough Station, and front entrance STL959 waits its turn on the 442 route. For over a year, later on in its life, it was the First Aid Hut at Hemel Hempstead Garage.

New Oxford Street and green liveried ST1101 working from Middle Row Garage, again shows off the square cab of these vehicles.

(left) One of only two T's from the first batch of 50 to carry a rounded cab as opposed to the normal square finished product. T45 clearly shows this oddity off, though lacking any other details as to its home garage or to the route it might next be used on. (J.H. Aston)

(below) Hardly used TD76 at Kingston Station shows off the clean lines of its Mann Egerton bus body mounted on a Leyland PS 1 chassis, and classified 1/1TD2 by the Executive. (J.H. Aston)

(right) SRT2 under the Park Royal body of which lies the chassis of ex STL2520, the body was later used in the build of RT4440.

(below) RT65 and STL1854 share the stand here at Morden Underground Station. The STL was one of the original "tunnel" buses, but by the time this photograph was taken, had received a standard LPTB body, albeit missing its roof box. (J.H. Aston)

Photographed inside Chiswick Works is Bluebird LT1425 which at this time was recorded as a learner bus, used by Reigate garage. All that I can say, is what a magnificent looking beast, but it is unlikely it actually worked on route 410 unless anyone knows different? (J.C. Gillham)

Square cabbed ST1129 painted green, helps out on route 35 in this photograph. It is seen working from its last operational garage, which is Camberwell, being scrapped in the first month of 1950 by Daniels of Rainham.

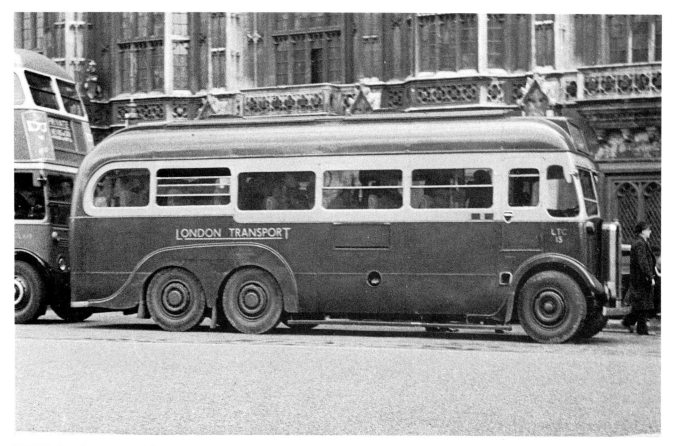

LTC15 clearly powered by an oil engine as evidenced by the protruding radiator and sheet metal work required to fill the gap. When fitted with a petrol engine the back of the radiator sat right up flush with the front of the bodywork. This was an example of a body without the roof observation glass panels. (S.N.J. White)

Q62 caught half in the shade, but clearly showing the frontal appearance given to these 4Q4 vehicles. The rather unusual blind shows the circular nature of route 425. This bus finished its life at an unknown oil refinery during 1953, having been resold by Norths (Dealer) of Leeds to whom it was disposed of by LTE. (A.B. Cross)

Brand new Park Royal bodied RTL150 shows to good advantage the lovely finish to the paint work enjoyed in this era. (J.H. Aston)

(above) A fine looking bus is STL2657 one of only three 17STL17, delivered in 1941 and which lasted till 1950 in passenger revenue earning service. Photographed here before being used as a training vehicle, then staff bus, before disposed of. (J.H. Aston)

(right) A Classic 60 seater STL on one of the routes associated with these fine looking vehicles, working from Turnham Green garage. (A.B. Cross)

T219 now preserved by the London Transport Museum at Covent Garden, this view shows the vehicle in green livery on central area duties at Well Hall Station, Eltham. Converted during the War to a staff ambulance it subsequently received a bus type front indicator which has been removed again in the course of restoration. (A.B. Cross)

Acquired by the Board from London General Omnibus Company, STL167 is a further example with LGOC 60 seat bodywork. This bus was scrapped just two months after this photograph was taken. (D.W.K. Jones)

From left to right LT675, TD11 and TD30 together with an RT in the background make up this view taken from Hampden Road of Muswell Hill Garage. (D.W.K. Jones)

LT34 leads a brace of ST's up onto the Epsom Downs, having made the journey from Morden Underground Station. This trip must have been one of its last as it was unlicensed the following month, for scrapping by Daniels. (Lens of Sutton)

STL322 and SRT42 stand at Arnos Grove Station awaiting their turn on route 84. The route information blind boxes have not changed much, considering the difference in years separating build of these two buses. (A.B. Cross)

A nice shot of Q107, one of a batch of 80 such vehicles coded 5Q5 built for both the country area and central area. Bodywork was by Park Royal, and seating provided for 37 passengers, though this was altered during the war years to allow a greater number of standing passengers, the original layout was reintroduced in post-war years. (A.B. Cross)

Standing at Bromley-by-Bow is Q170 which was one of those included in the first batch of 5Q5's to be disposed of in 1953.

LT684 operating on the special service for the Wimbledon Tennis fans and photographed at Wimbledon Railway Station. Luckily the bus was photographed the same month as it was scrapped so I suppose this was one of its last duties to perform.

Front entrance STL1032 waiting for business at West Croydon Station. A few years away from being disposed of to W. and C. French (contractors) of Buckhurst Hill, via North the dealers of Leeds. (A.B. Cross)

Camden Gardens terminus provides a resting place for ST462 in this summer shot. Perhaps it needs the rest, as it was scrapped before the end of the year. Interesting locomotive power is visible behind on the North London line.

Wartime delivered Brush bodied D52 working from Merton Garage on route 65 which was an unusual Bank Holiday duty, contrasts sharply with a post-war delivered RT pictured behind. (Lens of Sutton)

(left) LT1078 a superb rear end view of a single-deck LT of the type with rear indicator box, clearly showing the emergency exit arrangements for the passengers of the time. The Queen Victoria Pub at North Cheam is the setting for this view.
(A.B. Cross)

(below) Broad Street Station and ST372 looks in quite good condition, may be due to the fact that it had been overhauled by Berkeley Caravans of Biggleswade the previous year. (J.H. Aston)

(above) A fine view of STL594 in Gracechurch Street, with Chiswick built 56 seat body, known as the leaning-back variety because of the pronounced slope to the front of these vehicles. (J.H. Aston)

(right) Behind Putney Bridge Garage ST868B, now used as a learner vehicle, takes a rest from its arduous task of helping train new drivers for London Transport. During part of World War II, it was loaned to Crosville Motor Services of Chester. (A.B. Cross)

RT's nearing completion, photographed inside the building, used by the Saunders Shipbuilding & Engineering Company, of Beaumaris, Anglesey. Incidently the building still stands to this day and is used in the construction of lorry bodies by the Laird (Anglesey) Limited organisation. (Saunders)

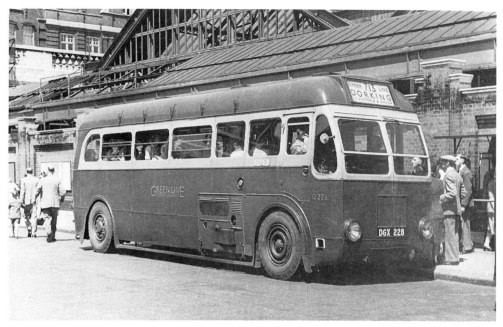

Built in 1937 as a Green Line coach and photographed in this same capacity on Eccleston Bridge is Q222c, the c indicating coach as opposed to the b which some vehicles carried standing for bus. Interestingly, although route board information brackets are fitted, no board is carried. (A.B. Cross)

ST387 was loaned to the Caledonian Omnibus Company, of Dumfries for sometime in excess of two and a half years during World War II, then overhauled by Berkeley Caravans, Biggleswade in December 1948, only to be scrapped by Daniels, of Rainham in January 1950.

Golders Green Underground Station and STD51 waits for its duty on the 183 route. These buses, although an all Leyland product, bore a similar resemblance to the roof box STL of the same period. (J.C. Gillham)

Just days after entering service, TD63 is photographed at Windmill Lane, Greenford. It carries a Mann Egerton bus body seating 31; the complete vehicle being coded 1/1TD2 as were all 100 of this combination of chassis and body. (J.C. Gillham)

STD138 in accompaniment with STD161 at the Green Man, Leytonstone. An all Leyland product these 4STD3 buses represented the first post-war type of double-deck vehicles purchased by the Board after World War II, even before the RT Class began to arrive in their thousands.

(J.C. Gillham)

Photographed prior to making its way up to the Scottish Omnibus Group in 1951 is G78, a Park Royal bodied variety, seen here at Golders Green Underground Station. (J.C. Gillham)

(left) Park Royal bodied RT724 waits in the sunshine at Hampton Court on the Sunday only Willesden Garage (AC) operation of route 112.

(J.H. Aston)

(below) A lovely photograph of proud looking STL263, having pulled through the war years and never needing to be rebuilt or renovated. Sadly only four months service is left, but at Bromley North terminus, looks as if it has many years work to do.

(A.B. Cross)

(*above*) Another brand new bus in this case, RT2274, having been put into service with no advertisements to mar its Weymann body. (J.H. Aston)

(*right*) Park Royal bodied G148 originally a 1/3G8 photographed here at Golders Green Underground Station. This bus was one of number which operated for W. Alexander and Sons, Falkirk in later years. (J.H. Aston)

In the grounds of Saunders Shipbuilding & Engineering Company, can be seen RT chassis awaiting their turn to have bodies built on them. The chassis are easily identifiable as being those with no chassis extensions beyond the rear wheels. In this photograph there is a batch of RT chassis to the left, in the middle of the picture stand four left-hand drive A.E.C. Regal Mark III's, and to the right are further RT type chassis. (Saunders)

Windmill Lane, Greenford is where STD157 stands, with less than a year to go before it gets its first overhaul with London Transport. (J.H. Aston)

Another ST, this time ST655, in Whitehall shows off its Berkeley Caravans overhauled bodywork to good advantage.

LT349 another of the class used for the Epsom Races in June. It appears earlier in the book when on Route 12. (Lens of Sutton)

LT187 photographed in March, standing in Windmill Lane, Greenford with only 10 months more service left to do, before going to Daniels (dealer), Rainham for scrapping. (J.C. Gillham)

An ex Bucks Expresses (Watford) Limited coach T391, was originally known as T307, when working for Green Line Coaches Limited way back in 1933. It was renumbered by LPTB in 1935, as there was already an ex Thomas Tilling vehicle carrying this number. (D.W.K. Jones)

LT668 and an interesting background in this photograph, with the delivery tricycle and the pedestrian marching along, one wonders if he has recently been demobbed from the Services with that distinctive stride they had to use.

Photographed at the Aldwych, ST146 shows to good advantage what the offside of this type of ST looked like. Like others of the class it was painted grey for service along routes which served sensitive wartime areas during World War II.

RT2258 painted in green livery was one of the batch of such liveried vehicles which were temporary used in the central fleet for a couple of months from new before being transferred to the Country Area. (J.H. Aston)

Green Line T622 on a private hiring to the races, shows no sign of its operational base, which at the time was Tring (TG) Garage. (J.H. Aston)

LTC3 before being fitted with an oil engine to replace its petrol variety in 1950. These were fine looking Weymann bodied 6 wheelers for their time, having been built in the late 1930s. (J.H. Aston)

(*left*) LT1167 one of many single deck LT's to be renovated by Marshall's of Cambridge between December 1948 and February 1949 and photographed some eight months later. Compare the condition to that of LT1068.

(*below*) G43, the lone Duple bodied example, ended its days in Yugoslavia along with many others from the G class.

(A.B. Cross)

LT1428 one of only two single deck LTs acquired from London General Country Services of Reigate, both of which were repainted red during the war years. (A.B. Cross)

The Menai Bridge forms the background to RT1158 just out from the paint shop, with all necessary operators transfers, and the John Bull advertising found on many buses of the era. Only route blinds are required before the bus can go into service. (Saunders)

Daniels yard at Rainham with LT1278 in the foreground. Are there any ghosts of the many London buses and coaches which ended their life here, one wonders!

Another view of mobile canteen 689J shows very clearly the outside stair arrangement of an ex Thomas Tilling bus. Also of note is the 20 m.p.h. restriction plate which was presumably necessary because of its registration as a good vehicle. (J.H. Aston)

Photographed at New Eltham Station is STL188, the body of which was built by the L.G.O.C. at Chiswick Works and was one of those that seated 60 passengers.

LT457 appears to have had some attention to its body panels, otherwise there seems no other explanation as to why the name London Transport appears to have a darker background.

STL376 now demoted to learner duties from its revenue earning days had only two more months left with the Executive when this photograph was taken. (A.B. Cross)

The roof line is clearly visible on another view of a tunnel bus, this time STL834, seen here pulling up the slope at the south end of Blackwall Tunnel. This vehicle was out of the general tunnel STL sequence and was rebuilt in 1944. Note the non-opening front windows. (C. Carter)

Dorking bus garage provides the stand here for TF44 in full dress for the journey to Baker Street via Kingston.

Another view of a fine looking 10T10, in this case T691 and photographed in Crawley, a long way from its home garage at Amersham. (S.E. Letts)

B26 with TD64 parked up behind in Windmill Lane, Greenford in March of this year. B26 worked its whole life from Hanwell Garage, but TD64 moved around the system. (J.C. Gillham)

Parked behind Putney Bridge Garage (F) both LT426 and ST152 are now demoted to learner duties. ST152 is in green livery, originally being operated by National Omnibus and Transport Company Limited on behalf of London General Omnibus Company in the early thirties.

Piccadilly Circus, looking up Shaftesbury Avenue and in this photograph only RT and STL type buses are to be seen. (London Transport 15568)

G326 a Park Royal bodied variety, delivered earlier in the year to Upton Park garage in red and broken white livery, as opposed to the brown livery that many were put into service with during the war years. Viewed at East Ham Town Hall. (A.B. Cross)

Photographed at Blomfield Street prior to turning into Liverpool Street, is ST822, having been overhauled by Berkeley Caravans of Biggleswade during July and August 1948. The bus went on to do a couple of months as a trainer at Willesden Garage after it had finished operating in service from Dalston Garage.

(left) Victoria Station forecourt, and all around STL835 are various buses. A photographers paradise.

(A.B. Cross)

(below) STL1048 one of a number known as the "Godstone" type of STL with interesting lowbridge front entrance Weymann bodies. Seen here at the Bromley North Station terminus of route 410. (A.B. Cross)

(above) For 18 months during World War II, ST572 was loaned to South Shields Corporation, but now waits for business at Morden Underground Station, having only a few more months service left with London Transport.

(right) Weymann bodied G407 picks up a hefty load from the opposite side of the road to the Royal Forest Hotel, Chingford. Typifying the day-outing by bus, popular in the period.

Photographed at Victoria, long before the complete change of character which has now taken place at this terminus. RT, STD and ST Class vehicles keep LT491 company alongside the original LGOC despatcher's tower.

ST920, LT35 and T264 waiting their turn to be scrapped, with so many others in the background. (A.B. Cross)

I hope you have enjoyed this collection of photographs covering the varied types of buses and coaches which once were used in the fleet of London Transport circa 1949.

I have had great pleasure in assembling this book and look forward to seeing you in my forth coming publication 'LONDON TRANSPORT, Buses and Coaches in 1950'.